Doors into Prayer

Doors into Prayer

An Invitation

EMILIE GRIFFIN

PARACLETE PRESS
Brewster, Massachusetts

2005   First Trade Paperback Printing
2001   First Hardcover Printing

Copyright © 2001 by Emilie Griffin

ISBN 1-55725-456-7

Library of Congress Cataloging-in-Publication Data
Griffin, Emilie.
    Doors into prayer : an invitation / Emilie Griffin.
        p. cm.
Includes bibliographical references (p. 113–119).
    ISBN 1-55725-456-7
1. Prayer—Christianity. I. Title.
BV210.2 .G7432 2001
248.3'2—dc21   2001004100

PARACLETE PRESS
Brewster, Massachusetts
www.paracletepress.com

Printed in the United States of America

For my grandson
David Ardis Sikes
Who at ten weeks old has already
taught me something about prayer

≈

Contents

PART ONE *Invitations*

PART TWO *Exercises*

Foreword

....

WHEN I WAS FIRST *learning to pray, I always had some book or other in my coat pocket, in my briefcase, one that would help me to pray in the middle of things.* Doors into Prayer *is meant to be like that: a brief introduction to the life of prayer, to be sampled at random moments throughout the day. This book means to capture the basics of prayer and the practicalities of a disciplined prayer life.*

Essentially, there are two ways to invite you to the life of prayer. The first is to give some general instructions and encouragements about praying: how it's done, what the methods are, and so forth. These are just techniques, but it's valuable to know them. They do make prayer concrete for us. The second way is to describe or sketch out or dramatize the experience of prayer. The danger is that no one's experience is ever, fully, like anyone else's, so intimate is the connection between God and each one of us. But even so, we are encouraged by such hints and glimpses of the interior life. So I will offer some descriptions of my own.

In Part One I'll provide short reflections on types of prayer, ways of praying, and prayer experience seen from the inside. I call these short discussions "invitations," for that is my intent. I hope you'll find them light reading. Each one should flow easily to the next. I also hope that you can stop at any given point and start to pray, if you feel so inclined. The value in reading Part One straight through is that you get an overview. Then you may go back to reflect on certain passages for a deeper understanding of prayer. In Part Two I will offer some structured exercises for prayer. At the end I'll make some suggestions for further reading.

That's the plan. Yet the text itself is meant to be open, in the sense that you can dip in any time and just about anywhere.

My aim is to open some doors into prayer. So this brief work is less about method and more about possibilities. It is meant as a book about God and us: about God's warm invitation to us, and our mysterious reluctance to accept. Is fear what holds us back? Or the deadly sin called world-weariness, a kind of lassitude or boredom that keeps us from getting involved? The solution of course is in the praying, the will to belong to God and choosing to be in God's presence. You'll find mentions of the relentless hunger of prayer, the elusiveness of God, observations on discouragement and doubt, hints about consolation. My hope is that you will often put the book down and pray; mend the ragged edges of your own prayer-life; start again, if you've been away from God; continue, if you haven't been away from God. Above all, may you open up to the splendor.

Emilie Griffin
Alexandria, Louisiana
May 4, 2001

Invitations

Emergencies

....

SOME OF US ARE TAUGHT to pray in childhood. We learn to memorize prayers and to
recite them. I have in mind the image, in A.A.
Milne's book, of Christopher Robin at bedtime:
"Hush! Hush! Whisper who dares! Christopher
Robin is saying his prayers."[1] But perhaps in this
happy bedtime experience, being fussed over
and tucked in by a devoted parent or grand-
parent, we don't fully learn to pray.

What comes later and with some force is fear.
We feel insecure, off balance. At such times we
are blessed if the childhood teaching sustains us.
But even if it doesn't, we find we can pray in
emergencies. Without much formality, the
words come.

I remember being in Mexico City during a
major earthquake that struck in the night.
People wandered from their beds, crying out,
finding the doorways in the dark and telling
others what to do. "Go into the doorway, it's the
safest place," someone called out to me. And
when I found myself in the doorway, not yet

safe but safe enough to take stock of what was happening, I knew I was praying, and had already been praying for some seconds. (Earthquakes are measured in seconds, but they feel much longer.) In emergencies we want clearheadedness, confidence, steady nerves. And so, without much coaching, we pray.

When Jesus and his followers were being tossed around by a fierce storm on the sea of Galilee, Jesus slept through it. The others could not. When they roused him to calm the storm for them, what they wanted most was stability. But Jesus offered them serenity. He criticized them for their lack of prayer. "Oh you little-faith-ers!" When we pray in emergencies, we exercise faith without thinking about it. There's no time for doubt now, something tells us. Consistent with the time-honored view that there are no atheists in foxholes, we cry out to a power greater than ourselves. Inwardly or outwardly we shout for help. No one has to tell us how to pray.

Is there a lesson here? Elaborate schemes and civilized styles of prayer may exist, but the need to pray is primitive and fundamental. Prayer is built into us, as it were, ready to flow when trouble kicks in. Admittedly, such prayers are

4

fleeting. If we pray in emergencies, and only then, we can hardly say we have a relationship to God. But the prayer of emergencies tells us, without question, that such a relationship is possible.

Wonder

....

ANOTHER WAY PRAYER begins is in wonder. From early childhood we have a sense of the sacred, but we don't know how to give it a name. I remember, at about age three, being amazed by sunlight filtering through my eyelashes. I was astonished by the way the prisms on our Victorian lamp could throw rainbows on the floor. All around me, when I was small, were experiences of wonder. With neighborhood playmates I learned to catch dragonflies, not to harm them, but to hear them buzz, watch their wings tremble, observe their color, then to let them go again, throwing them out onto currents of air, where they got their balance and flew away. I liked to watch small lizards throw back their red throats and puff them out. We children said they were "showing their money." Ordinary flowers in our back garden pleased me: petunias, nasturtiums, pansies, snapdragons. These moments of awe may be embedded deep in memory. When the American writer and Cistercian monk Thomas Merton was about five years old, he had a moment of grace. Outdoors with his father on a Sunday morning, he heard church bells, and saw birds flying, and he said: "Father, all the birds are in their church." And then: "Why don't we go to church?"[2] C.S. Lewis describes a stab of childhood yearning beside a currant bush on a summer day. He felt something keenly, but did not know how to name it. As he grew older, he called it by the German word *Sehnsucht* and by the English word "joy," but giving "joy" a specialized meaning. Only after many years was he able to connect this experience with the presence of God. What he felt was sacredness and power. Many primitive peoples have sacred places, groves where the presence of a god is felt. Perhaps they have honored this experience more than we do.[3]

Such an experience of joy and praise may come in a flash, without warning. At last we guess that God is speaking to us with love. We begin to express our love in return. Our hearts leap up, as Wordsworth says, when we behold a rainbow in the sky.

Longing

....

PERHAPS WE HAVE LEARNED about formal prayer, and practiced it, without ever connecting it to that odd, uneasy longing that drives us continually toward the Ultimate. We spend our days and nights in a vague loneliness for some-one or something to make us feel complete. Many people divert this longing into kinds of self-gratification, hoping to still the restlessness. Yet even though we chase down blind alleys, this drive (I suspect it is toward God) continues to move us inwardly. Though we may not yet know how to speak of God, still we are moved by our heartache. "The heart has its reasons," said Pascal.[4] Evelyn Underhill speaks of such a yearning as "Godsickness," akin to homesick-ness, the push toward an unnamed destiny.[5] "Our hearts are restless," Augustine says, "until they rest in You."[6]

The longing to pray is in itself a kind of prayer. Awkwardly felt, not well-shaped, and often misunderstood, this wanting seems to be no more than a lack, or better described, a hunger. The hunger is a blessing but we may not know it. Jesus must have guessed that people felt awkward about their godly yearnings. To comfort them he said, as we read in Matthew 5:6, "Blessed are those who hunger and thirst for righteousness, for they shall be filled."

Dorothy Day spoke of her search for God as a long loneliness. Certainly, she longed and yearned for God until at last she found the one she was looking for.[7] Once we have become people of prayer, people who are comfortable with praying, even so, many of our prayers express no more than simple longing: "As a deer longs for flowing streams," Psalm 42 says, ". . . so my soul longs for you, O God." Psalm 77 is even more vehement: "I cry aloud to God, aloud to God, that he may hear me." And in Psalm 84, "My soul longs, indeed it faints for the courts of the LORD."

Many of our stories of looking for God are stories of unease, of wandering. I remember myself as a young Manhattanite, surrounded by topless towers and blown by cold winds along dusty streets, popping into churches now and again because I found them comfortable places, places where meaning reigned secure. Yet the hymn I often hummed under my breath was that American folk song, "I wonder as I wander out under the sky."

Structure

....

ONCE YOU HAVE DECIDED that you want not just random prayer but a *life* of prayer, you have come to the point where a structure is needed. However much you love to be spontaneous and laid-back, never fenced in by due dates, you must sketch out some kind of schedule for prayer.

So many activities and concerns press in on us. So many friends and strangers demand long and short stretches of our time. If we are to develop a real relationship to God, we should set aside time, and congenially, in ways that do not require superhuman effort. We must develop time and space for God within an already over-scheduled life.

At first it sounds both impractical and arrogant, to schedule time for God, but maybe we are scheduling time for ourselves, rather than for God. This time will permit us to enjoy God's company and know God's love.

No doubt we will make it much more difficult than it has to be. We will stack up many spiritual books to be sure of filling the time. We will acquire prayer journals and books about how to use prayer journals. Mind you, I'm not against either books or journals. I would heartily recommend both. But they shouldn't complicate matters. The idea is to come into God's presence without much fanfare, on a regular schedule, with simplicity.

I know a university chaplain who has marked off two mornings a week on his calendar. These are his times to reflect and to pray. A friend of mine established a prayer group that meets once a month, in which each person has an opportunity to design an evening of prayer for the others, choosing Scriptures and readings and allowing for quiet time. A mother at home with young children may find her best prayer time comes after the school bus has left. A working mother may schedule in a prayer time after she leaves the day-care center and before she gets to the office; but is the car really an environment for prayer? Automobile prayers have their limits; but sometimes they are the best we can do.

My own practice has changed over the years. When I was younger, and working in New York City, I went to church almost every morning.

My spiritual life was structured around that. Sometimes I would go into a church at lunchtime, to pray fifteen minutes, sometimes longer. I would make the occasional retreat. Later on, while working at a fast-paced office in New Orleans, I found myself not far from a formal garden where flowers were in bloom year-round. On lunch hours I took refuge in this peaceful place. Often, to create an environment for prayer, one must break with the routine and be creative. A walk or a drive may relieve our daily pressures. We gain a sense of freedom from the time we give to God.

Self-Giving

....

BY NOW I AM SURE you have noticed that you can't really study prayer from the outside. You can't be a scientific researcher, put prayer under a microscope, make a list of your observations, and say, "Oh, now I understand prayer." As long as you are on the outside, looking in, you really don't know anything about prayer. You have to give yourself to prayer.

Really, praying is a little bit like a parachute jump. There is preparation, but there are no trial runs. The first time counts. You can watch a lot of training films, but then, you have to take the chance. Then it's the real thing: prayer.

So that's the first thing about prayer: giving ourselves. That self-giving is fundamental, the common thread that runs through all the different kinds of prayer. Even when we are praying for somebody else, using intercessory prayer, we are giving ourselves to the prayer. It is an act of the will, an intention, from the Latin word meaning "to stretch toward." "Please, Lord," we say, "listen to me; Lord, hear my prayer. Bring me into your presence, Lord." When we make an intention, when we stretch toward God and whatever else we aim for, we are giving ourselves to God. That is the beginning of prayer.

A Prayer-Mentor

IN DESIGNING OUR PRAYER LIVES we may look to others as examples. One of my prayer-mentors has been the British writer C.S. Lewis, who in the middle of university teaching and writing was a devoted and creative person of prayer. How did he plan his time to include both prayer and worship? His schedule is well documented. On weekdays he attended services in his college chapel. He sometimes went to weekday services at a nearby church. On Sundays he went to a church near his home. On Thursday evenings in his college rooms he met with a circle of friends, who were as keen on God as he was. Over and above this, he pursued certain friendships of the heart. J.R.R. Tolkien was one such friend. Charles Williams was another. Jesus, one could say, was an unseen third in their twosomes. And Lewis engaged in private prayer. He prayed in odd places, not always quiet places. He was fond of praying on railway journeys. He liked long walks. When he was alone, these were good chances for prayer.

Reflecting on Lewis as a spiritual mentor was helpful for me. He was certainly scheduled to the hilt! Even so, he managed to pray, in both formal and informal ways. Studying his life, and the lives of others in his circle, helped me to see friendship as an aspect of spiritual life. We share our love of God with others, and God is present with us when we do.

Jesus

....

CONSIDER JESUS as a resource for our lives of prayer. Shaped by a culture and a home life that reinforced prayer, Jesus probably took part in formal worship at least three different times a day. The everyday things he did were accompanied by prayer.

But apparently Jesus couldn't get enough of prayer. Even with prayer as the common practice of the culture he lived in, Jesus still looked for times of quiet and solitude. Scripture shows him often in solitary prayer. "In the morning, when it was still very dark, he got up and went out to a deserted place, and there he prayed. And Simon and his companions hunted for him" (Mark 1:35–36). ". . . he made his disciples get into the boat and go on ahead to the other side, to Bethsaida, while he dismissed the crowd. [Then] . . . he went up onto the mountain to pray" (Mark 6:45–46). "After he had dismissed the crowds, he went up the mountain by himself to pray. When evening came, he was there alone" (Matt.14:23). Luke tells in chapter 5 of his

Gospel that, as the word spreads and the crowds gather, Jesus goes to deserted places to pray. Worn out from his public ministry, and from dealing with the scribes and the Pharisees, he goes up the mountain and spends the whole night in prayer. In Luke 9, Jesus is praying alone, and then he goes up onto the mountain to pray; soon his companions find him transfigured by contact with God.

These are just a few citations. But they help us to know that for Jesus, prayer wasn't a random activity. It was the way he lived, which is what some spiritual writers call "union with God." (Union is a kind of connectedness, being with God all the time.) Jesus wanted others to live this way. He meant for us to enter the reign of God here and now. When we look at prayer the way Jesus did, we are looking at something large and freeing. Our whole lives can become prayer.

Spiritual Reading

OFTEN OUR PRAYER includes spiritual reading. Recently I heard from a husband and wife, married more than fifty years, how their spiritual lives are planned. After breakfast each morning, they have devotional time, in which they read short selections from several different sources. First they use a daily Scripture passage and a one-page devotional thought for the day. Next they read a chapter or so from the New Testament or the Psalms, without notes or helps. Then each one reads from favorite spiritual anthologies. After this, they spend about fifteen to twenty minutes in silent prayer. Partly this is prayer of intercession; each one has a list of people and things to pray for, and they pray for the sick among their acquaintances. They spend some time in thanksgiving; they pray for people whose spiritual needs are known to them; they pray for various spiritual leaders and pastors, and for causes affecting Christian life. Finally, they spend some time praying for their own needs. In silence, they listen to God.

After hearing about this prayer schedule, I decided that one of the blessings of getting older is having more time for prayer. I laughed when the husband, reporting on this prayer time, mentioned that he'd like to become more regular about meditation: "I don't do this nearly as often as I wish to!" But to me it sounded like a large commitment of time, larger than most of us can manage.

Spiritual reading is not the same as active study of a text. When we read as part of our prayer, we want God to draw us into a closer relationship. We are not striving to master the text, but to be led by it. Soon the line between reading and praying starts to disappear. We cross the boundary when we begin to speak to God or let God speak to us. Sometimes we hardly know when we have moved from reading to prayer.

Attentiveness

....

*T*HE ESSENCE OF PRAYER is to give God our full attention. Often, our lives are so scattered, our attention so fractured, that the simple task of being attentive is a way of being healed. We relearn, in prayer, the simple attentiveness of a child.

Recently, I've seen my grandson, who is ten weeks old, noticing things. He becomes entranced with something on the ceiling. He notices the bright colors of books in a bookcase. He is totally caught up in his mother's or his father's face. Can we recapture the full attentiveness we once knew in childhood? Yes, when we are fully absorbed in God.

To do this we must let go of the accumulated cares and concerns, the busyness and fragmentation of our daily existence. We set everything else aside and come into the presence of God. When we do this, even briefly, God overtakes our scattered lives and focuses them once again. Attentiveness to God is a healing thing.

People in simpler societies pray with their work. They find God gracing them in their work. Thus, from the heritage of earlier times, we hear of prayers of the anvil and prayers of the loom. Such prayers of simple, repetitive work—the prayer of folding the laundry, the prayer of peeling the potatoes, the prayer that ascends with steam from the tea-kettle—these prayers of a simpler culture are reminders to us. Attention and simplicity call us back to what is real. Attention is the beginning of prayer; in a sense it is both the beginning and end of prayer, to focus our attention on God.

Prayer-Scapes

....

THE PLACES WHERE WE GO to pray can sometimes make a difference. They lead us into prayer. In gardens, or on country walks, we may see God's power in a tree, a ray of sunlight, a flowing stream. Natural beauty opens us up to prayer because of the connections we make: God has crafted all this loveliness, we say. Shakespeare speaks of this: "Sermons in stones," he says, "and good in everything."[8] But sometimes we may choose prayer-scapes because they challenge us.

Once, when considering the question of economic power, I spent a day of reflection in Lower Manhattan. My prayer-scapes were somewhat unusual: the New York Stock Exchange, the church where George Washington often prayed, even Fraunces Tavern, where Washington said farewell to his officers. My hope for the retreat was to appreciate the American experience and to reflect on how the unique aspects of American power might be put to good purposes.

Dorothy Day is said to have prayed in and through the city, seeing Christ in the faces of the poor.

Consider a more elaborate pilgrimage: to Gettysburg, the Vietnam War Memorial, the Holocaust Museum. We can suit our prayer-scapes to our prayer intentions. Or we can let the place itself shape our prayers. Sometimes the relentless noise and bustle of the city provide us with a call to prayer, or possibly concerns about justice or poverty come to us more strongly there.

Familiar Prayers

....

ALMOST EVERYONE LEARNS certain prayers
by rote, or as we say, "by heart." These are the
prayers we recite hastily in times of stress. The
Lord's Prayer is certainly one of these prayers
which is not only common knowledge but, as it
were, second nature. We say it, sometimes we
rattle through it, because we know it so well.

Yet familiar prayers can become the starting
point of much deeper praying. One way to go
about this is to take a familiar prayer and slow it
down. "Our Father," we say, and then spend a
time of silent reflection, savoring the depth and
the meaning, before moving on to the well-
known words, "who art in heaven." By taking
such a prayer and slowing it down, we begin to
pray at another level of meaning. The power of
God flows into us. We make space for God within us.

Other familiar prayers may lend themselves
to this slowed-down depth of intention and
meaning. One of these is Mary's prayer, "My
soul magnifies the Lord," often called by its

Latin name, "The Magnificat." Of course, this is only one of the biblical prayers known as canticles. All the canticles lend themselves to this deeply attentive praying and, because of their content and structure, will give both shape and meaning to our prayer.

You may want to consider returning to some long-forgotten prayer of childhood: "Now I lay me down to sleep" is one of these. Often one of the best ways to pray is with prayers already committed to memory, because the memory-strand, which is already part of our consciousness, permits us to weave in a new, fresh strand of prayer over one which already exists. In doing this we are both learning prayer and relearning it.

Recollection

....

RECOLLECTION IS A DOORWAY into prayer. It is a kind of focus to arrive at tranquility. This useful practice goes by different names. Sometimes it is called "centering." Richard Foster mentions that the Quakers call it "centering down." Brother Lawrence of the Resurrection speaks of "the practice of the presence." Still another expression is "going within."[9]

An exercise for recollection may go something like this: Right where you are, sit up straight. Put down your notebook, your pencil or anything you have to hold. Make sure your spine is completely straight. Now, relax. Gather yourself in, so to speak. Be completely together in the place where you are. Let any stress or anxiety slide away. Be at peace. Now feel the light of God's presence shining on you, feel God's blessing coming upon you. Accept that blessing. Then breathe in deeply and breathe out deeply. Take one or two breaths, feel the rhythm of it. Next, speak to the Lord, inwardly. You might say to God silently, "Speak, Lord, your servant is listening." Now we have come to the doorway. We are recollected and ready to pray, in fact, we have already begun to pray.

Recollection is a good space to be in at any time. We can move into prayer, or out of prayer, when we are in a recollected state. Recollecting or centering provides an inward attentiveness, or focus, which is essential to all prayer. This practice of gentle concentration moves us into tranquility and peace.

Prayer of the Heart

....

THIS ANCIENT FORM of easygoing prayer, which can be traced to the earliest days of Christianity, is very adaptable to contemporary life. Sometimes called "prayer of the heart," this simplest of all forms of contemplation offers a practical approach to the love of Christ on a daily and comfortable basis.

But it is not prayer of effort: quite the reverse. Prayer of the heart is simple prayer of the easy yoke and the light touch. Come to me, Jesus says, all you who are weighed down with cares and troubles, and I will refresh you and give you rest.

Praying with the heart means going deeper than just thinking or intellectualizing or recitation.

A beneficial technique, taught as part of the prayer of the heart, is to pray in concert with the breath. Of course this is very ancient. In both Hebrew and Latin the word for "spirit" is close to the word for "breath." Breath is anciently associated with life.

If you breathe your prayer with a single word or phrase, you may soon be led into a more receptive state where you can hear or receive God's word to you, and be blessed by God's love.

Letting Go

....

WE OFTEN HEAR THAT the most important
aspect of prayer is "letting go." What does this
mean? Essentially, prayer is something we do by
relenting, by not trying too hard. "Be still," says
Psalm 46, "and know that I am God." Though
prayer requires attentiveness and concentration,
in another sense it should be effortless. For those
of us raised on an achievement-mentality, this
will take a little getting used to.

Well-intentioned prayer is not a matter of
striving for perfection. Because we have spent
much of our lives trying to earn love, to qualify
for approval, to deserve affection, we may now
have to unlearn our usual assumptions. Now we
must relax and let go, to be lifted on an ocean-
swell of grace.

God wants to draw us in. He wants us to
know his affection. Authentic prayer begins
when we turn ourselves over to the grace of
God. It is not a prayer of making requests, of
trying to get things done or figured out. This
kind of "resting in God" is not a matter of

doing, but of undoing. Resting in the love of the Spirit, we are sustained by the power of the living God.

Changes of Scene

....

SOMETIMES WE NEED a change of scene in order to pray. Studies have shown that a change of locale can heighten creativity. However it works, going to a different place, or perhaps an uncluttered space, clears the decks and focuses our concentration. Perhaps also we need privacy, and a sense of safety, in order to open up to God entirely. A different place may help, but our intention is more important. We want to focus on God, to be refreshed by the presence of God, to be led. By going to a different place, a safe place, we express that intention fully.

Solitude
and Silence

....

MUCH OF OUR PRAYER and worship is within a community. We sing hymns together. We voice prayers together. We build relationships with fellow believers. Yet sometimes our relationship with God can best be deepened by time spent alone. Some people find solitude more congenial than others. Not all of us are natural solitaries. But solitude is not yet prayer; it is a way into prayer. Solitude is a door.

When you open the door of solitude, you may find another door behind it. That is the door of silence. Silence, too, is an environment for prayer. In silence we put ourselves in touch with God and also with our deeper selves. Thoughts long buried come to the surface. Long-repressed feelings bubble up. Silence exposes certain issues in our lives, and almost without effort, what is most important comes to the forefront. Now we can place that "most important issue" before God as we pray.

The Still,
Small Voice

....

ORDINARY PEOPLE HAVE remarkable experiences in prayer. They hear God tenderly speaking to them in ways they can hardly describe. Sometimes, people are confused when they compare their own experiences to those in Scripture. The Bible stories are told in very bold strokes. God spoke to Moses in the burning bush, to our ancestors in the desert with pillars of fire. The experience of contemporary believers may not be so dramatic. Even so, a vivid relationship with God is possible, one in which God does most of the speaking and we do most of the listening.

Sometimes, by the way we pray, we do not allow for stillness. We are so busy with our complaints and our requests that we hardly stop to listen for the voice of God. Perhaps we think we are unworthy for God to speak to us, that God has better things to do. But how can the voice be heard, unless we listen? Sometimes God can hardly get a word in edgewise.

Often, we are told, the voice is still and small. Sometimes, when we are praying hard about a particular thing, no answer comes. Later, after the prayer time, in a different place, possibly the word will come to us. We need to be patient, as God has been patient with us.

God in Dialogue

....

CONSIDER HOW ABRAHAM prayed for the city of Sodom to be spared. He engaged in an up-front dialogue with God about the things that mattered most to him. In Genesis 18, Abraham's prayer is a form of negotiation. Granted that there are wicked people and practices in the city, but, Abraham asked, would God spare the city if fifty good people could be found there? Well, what about forty-five? Or forty? Or thirty? Or twenty? Or ten?

This passage in Genesis suggests a very rich relationship between Abraham and God. It's actually a description of the content of Abraham's prayer. Scripture often represents God in dialogue with us. The characters speak in rapid-fire exchanges. Our dialogue with God may be just as vigorous, but may not play out in a similar script. Every exchange is different and unique, and, whatever we may learn from Abraham's prayer, remember that God's word to us will be scripted for us and not for Abraham.

But we can expect that God will speak to us. So our listening should be razor-sharp. The God we believe in is personal, and engaged with us. We know the yearning that draws us to prayer; God's love is the reason for that yearning.

When we speak to God and stop to listen we may get a surprising reply.

Prayer as
Wrestling

....

I LIKE THAT PASSAGE in the story of Moses, in which God sends Moses to liberate the people of Israel, and Moses doesn't want to accept the call. This odd wrestling between Moses and God is mentioned in several different places. Moses responded to the Lord by saying, I'm not up to this challenge, this is more than I can handle.

"Then the LORD spoke to Moses, Go and tell Pharaoh King of Egypt to let the Israelites go out of his land. But Moses spoke to the LORD, 'The Israelites have not listened to me, how then shall Pharaoh listen to me, poor speaker that I am?'"(Exod. 6:10–12).

"On the day when the LORD spoke to Moses in the land of Egypt, he said to him, 'I am the LORD, tell Pharaoh king of Egypt all that I am speaking to you.' But Moses said in the LORD's presence, 'Since I am a poor speaker, why would Pharaoh listen to me?'"(Exod. 6:28–30).

In Exodus, chapter 4, God tells Moses what he is to do, in an extended dialogue. And everything Moses says is an expression, not only of his own inadequacy, but also of the implausibility of the huge mission that God has assigned to him.

Hear this out. Notice how long Moses continues to struggle. "But Moses said to God, 'If I come to the Israelites and say to them, "The God of your ancestors has sent me to you," and they ask me, "What is his name?" what shall I say to them?'"(Exod. 3:13).

And God gives him the words to say, but again, Moses objects, "Then Moses answered, 'But suppose they do not believe me or listen to me, but say, "The LORD did not appear to you. . . .""(Exod. 4:1).

And finally, when God keeps answering his doubts with specific wonders and signs, Moses says, "O my Lord, I have never been eloquent, neither in the past nor even now that you have spoken to your servant, but I am slow of speech and slow of tongue."

"Then the LORD said to him, 'Who gives speech to mortals? Who makes them mute or deaf, seeing or blind? Is it not I, the LORD? Now go, and I will be with your mouth and teach you what you are to speak.'"

And even after all this Moses says to the Lord, "O my Lord, please send someone else" (Exod. 4:13).

Even today, spiritual directors tell us, the content of a prayer may be authentically expressed in dialogue. "God said to me . . . I said to God" is our best way of telling how we met God and were led by the grace of the meeting.

Work

WE NOTICE IN SCRIPTURE that God seems to care about the ordinary things we do. Even our work can lead us closer to God. Do we really believe this? We have had a tendency to divide our work-lives from our home-lives and our prayer-lives. But work, that is, professional work, occupies a huge amount of our time. After we have come home from our professional work, there is still more work to do: kitchen duties, laundry, keeping our homes and belongings tidy and neat, washing and servicing the car, getting the motor vehicle license renewed, you name it. We can't afford to look at the majority of our time and call it secular, saying these activities belong to a world outside of God. We need God in all of our lives, in our work as in our rest and leisure.

If we take the right attitude and develop the right disposition, our prayer and our work can be intertwined. We can be conscious of God's blessing in everything we do. And our work can become prayer when we offer it to God. Paul writes in 1 Corinthians 10:31: "Whether you eat or drink, or whatever you do, do everything for the glory of God."

Anthony Bloom writes, "A prayer makes sense only if it is lived, if prayer and action are interwoven. . . ." Sometimes this prayer of everyday life and work is called the prayer of the ordinary.[10]

The philosopher-scientist Pierre Teilhard de Chardin says that God and the world come together right before our eyes, in the smallest detail of the work we do. Our work is God-given, Teilhard says, and so it follows that God will meet us in the least of our tasks. "God, in all that is most living and incarnate in Him, is not withdrawn from us beyond the tangible sphere; He is waiting for us at every moment in our action, in our work of the moment." But where? ". . . At the tip of my pen, my spade, my brush, my needle—of my heart and of my thought. By pressing the stroke, the line, or the stitch, on which I am engaged, to its ultimate natural fin-ish, I shall arrive at the ultimate aim towards which my innermost will tends."[11]

Prayer of
the Ordinary

HOW THEN SHOULD WE PRAY in the middle
of our work? While we are engaged in a particular action, we can make an intention, or a
prayer, in which we offer this action to God.
This was a common practice for earlier times.
The composer Johann Sebastian Bach wrote on
his musical scores, *Ad Soli Deo Gloria*, which
means "Glory be to God Alone." In the past,
schoolchildren and others scribbled a phrase on
their schoolwork: *Ad Majorem Dei Gloriam*,
sometimes abbreviated AMDG, which means
"to the greater Glory of God." These are little
ways people have sometimes used for offering
their work to God.

In Louisiana and Mississippi, the fishermen
ask for a blessing of the fleet. It is a formal cere-
mony in which the bishop comes to pray over
the shrimp boats and the oyster boats and the
nets, not too different from the way things
might have been on the shores of Galilee. At the

Prayer Channel, a television ministry in Brooklyn, New York, the effort began with a service for blessing the transmitters. Like the blessing of the boats, this too is a prayer of the ordinary. We say that the work is for the sake of God. We ask to be conscious of God's creative power manifested in ordinary things.

I had a neighbor in New York, who was Jewish. She told me how she had been in love with a young man from Israel, and she broke the engagement off because he prayed too much. "He had a prayer for every occasion," she said, "a prayer for getting on and off the bus, a prayer for going in and out of the house." Well, whether you approve of this young woman's decision or not, I think it makes a point. There will be times when we need to formalize our prayer, saying grace at table, praying together in church, or on certain occasions, but the prayer of the ordinary is not measured by the number of prayers that we say.

Surprises

....

PRAYING THE ORDINARY calls for a certain
attitude, an offering of the heart to God in our
simplest activities. When we arrange to pray
consistently at certain times, that spirit of prayer
will transform us inwardly. This inner disposition lets us receive God's blessing in and through
our work. We may become conscious of God's
love and mercy in surprising ways.

Simone Weil, the French philosopher and
mystic, tells the story of saying the Lord's Prayer
in Greek while picking grapes on a farm, a practice that led her into a very intense experience of
Jesus Christ.[12]

Janice Brewi, who is a mid-life counselor,
remembered a definitive moment in her own
life-crisis: "I was preparing string beans for a
meal. I had been doing spiritual reading during
the day. As I handled the beans I was drawn to
their texture: to look at their color, size, and
shape; to examine the ends as I clipped them off.
An overwhelming feeling of graciousness came
to me. I felt enveloped in goodness and love, all

emanating from the beans in my hands. I touched a bean to my face and lips in amazement. The bean signified for me my life, all of life, God's life. In those few instants, I knew that all was holy. All would work out for good."[13] Such an experience is pure gift. Janice Brewi did not set out to bless the beans. Instead, the beans blessed her! Possibly a sense of great blessing came at that moment, because she had been praying all along.

Examen

....

OUR CAPACITY TO RECEIVE this kind of blessing can be heightened and developed. Of
course, everyone is different. And everyone's
prayer is different. But everyone can use the
power of reflection to interpret the most commonplace events, from the morning sunlight to
the flat tire to the children's crayon-drawings on
the walls. What is God saying to us in these ups
and downs of daily existence?

The prayer of *examen* is an ancient prayer-
form by which we may specifically review a
given portion of the day, or the week, in order to
determine where we may have fallen from
grace, or more broadly, how God was specifically with us.

Plan to use the prayer of examen daily, before
or after lunch, or in the evening. First, give
thanks to God for all the graces you have
received, and try to name them: a telephone call
from a friend, flowers in bloom, a glimpse of
clouds or sky, a good laugh, something achieved
in your work. Doing this often brings a sense of

balance or consolation. Instead of reflecting on what we haven't received, we collect and gather in the blessings of the day. Also we may be able to pinpoint a challenge or notice a bad tendency that needs correction.

Whether or not we call it the prayer of examen, there is a real value in reflecting on the day's activities and seeing how God was present to us in any given time.

Heightened Consciousness

....

ESSENTIALLY THERE ARE two ways in which
our God-consciousness is heightened. The first
is prayer (in the broadest sense of an interaction
with God) and the second is reflection. When
we reflect on the ways God has been present to
us, we notice again, we are grateful again, we
heighten and deepen our experience of the
graces we have received.

So, there are several ways to pray through
everyday events: praying in and with particular
actions; receiving God's love in and with particular actions; using prayer to lift all our actions
to God; perceiving our own actions, even the
most mundane, as prayer (because we mean it
to be); reflecting deeply on the ways God is
already speaking to us. The more we do this,
the more we experience what Paul, the apostle,
calls unceasing prayer. In the words of David
Lonsdale, "What begins as a conscious effort to
look for signs of God in daily experience

gradually moves beyond conscious effort to a habitual way of seeing the world . . . and grasping the mystery of God in unexpected places."[14]

Daily Routine

....

RECENTLY I CAME ACROSS a written prayer which illustrates one good way to pray the ordinary. Composed by a major German theologian, Karl Rahner, it is called "God of My Daily Routine."[15] This prayer is ideal for those of us who feel hemmed in by a thousand daily responsibilities. How easy it is to suppose that God is far off, rather than right here in the middle of things with us.

I am struck by this lament: "My soul has become a huge warehouse where day after day the trucks unload their crates without any plan or discrimination, to be piled helter-skelter in every available corner and cranny, until it is crammed full from top to bottom with the trite, the commonplace, the insignificant, the routine . . . ." Rahner finds himself overwhelmed by "empty talk and pointless activity, idle curiosity and pretensions of importance that . . . roll forward in a never-ending stream."

Surely that is a predicament shared by many of us. But soon the prayer leads us past that predicament. "I now see clearly that, if there is any path at all on which I can approach you, it must lead through the middle of my ordinary daily life. . . .

"I must learn to have both 'everyday' and Your Day in the same exercise. In devoting myself to the works of this world, I must learn to give myself to You, to possess You, the one and only thing, in everything. . . . In You, all that has been scattered is reunited; in Your Love all the diffusion of the day's chores comes home again to the evening of Your unity. . . ."

I like this prayer. It reminds me that the Spirit of God comes to liberate me in the middle of everything. Things get dumped every day in the warehouse of my soul. Anxieties and interruptions get in the way. But then I notice that God is in the middle of the warehouse, giving me the strength to sort things out.

God's Pencils

SOMETIMES WRITTEN PRAYERS help us. They are so structured, so clear. They organize us and help us see how God is acting in our lives. And sometimes it is good to write our own prayers, or to pray with a pencil or pen in hand. As we pray, we write; or, better yet, the writing is the praying. Henri Nouwen spoke of writing as a journey into the unknown, one which would lead us to find surprising depths within ourselves. Paul Tournier, a Christian doctor and spiritual writer, commended writing as a form of prayer. Somehow, in my mind, I have connected the idea of writing a prayer with the famous saying of Mother Teresa of Calcutta. She called herself "God's pencil," an instrument of God's will.

Short Stabs
of Prayer

WHEN WE ARE RIGHT in the middle of things, how do we pray? Sometimes it is in little short stabs of prayer, the kind that my husband calls "short attention span prayers." "Dear Lord, have mercy on me," "Lord, can you help me with this?" "Lord, can you work with me here?" "Help thou my unbelief!" "I need you, God." "Dear Lord, come to my aid." Just a single short phrase spoken out loud or silently says it all; and sometimes, if we're in the middle of something requiring all our effort, that's all the prayer we can muster. Maybe it's all we need.

Little Ways

....

SOME PEOPLE ARE KNOWN for teaching this way of modest, unobtrusive prayer that connects with ordinary events. One is Brother Lawrence of the Resurrection, who wrote a small classic called *The Practice of the Presence of God*; two others are Thomas Kelly, who wrote *A Testament of Devotion,* and Frank Laubach, who wrote *Letters of a Modern Mystic*. A fourth person, Thérèse of Lisieux, had a way of praying with the ordinary things of life which is often called "The Little Way."

Their simple approach is to go through all our day's activities in awareness of God's presence. Brother Lawrence spent a lot of time working in the kitchen. He referred to himself as "the lord of pots and pans." His prayer method was therefore quite practical: "The time of business does not differ with me from the time of prayer; and in the noise and clatter of my kitchen, while several persons are at the same time calling for different things, I possess God in as great tranquility as if I were upon my knees at the blessed sacrament."[16] Now, possibly you are thinking, I can't do that all the time. And you're probably right. But you can do it some of the time. If you pray intensely part of the time, you may find that you come to pray more frequently—if not all of the time, then more of the time.

Kathleen Norris, in giving the Madaleva lecture at St. Mary's College in Notre Dame, Indiana, chose to speak on the ways that contemporary women can develop an authentic spirituality out of the our most uninspiring chores and challenges. Of course, women's work can be disheartening. But the fact is men face some pretty boring tasks as well. There is a lot of work that my husband calls "donkey work." A writer's work, he reminds me, is something like digging ditches.

But offering this kind of work and every kind of ditch-digging to God is what transforms that work. The poet Gerard Manley Hopkins said, "It is not only prayer that gives God glory but work. Smiting on an anvil, sawing a beam, whitewashing a wall, driving horses, sweeping, scouring, everything gives God some glory. . . . To lift up the hands in prayer gives God glory, but a man with a dungfork in his hand, a woman with a slop pail, give him glory too. God is so great that all things give him glory if you mean that they should."[17]

Well, the dungfork and the slop pail are the real extremes. And, of course, Hopkins was writing more than a century ago, in a rural environment. But his point holds good even now. The attitude we bring to work is what makes it more burdensome or less. Like Father Hopkins, like Brother Lawrence, like Thérèse of Lisieux, we can allow the power of God to transform our nights and days, to lift us up to new horizons.

Large-Scale Vision

FINDING GOD in the middle of a thousand small jobs and nuisances is good. Also, we need to step back sometimes and look at our lives as a whole. We should give ourselves credit for chipping away at the large-scale vocation to which God has called us. Periodically we need to enter things in the plus column, notice what we are accomplishing, what God is achieving through us. Prayer and reflection are ways to do this. Evelyn Underhill, the English mystical writer, says, "We ourselves form part of the creative apparatus of God."[18] God is doing his work through us, we are his hands and feet.

Imagination

....

PART OF WHAT WE DO in prayer is to conceive a God who wants to know us well. For many this is the most difficult stumbling block. Some find that scientific knowledge gets in the way of prayer. The universe is so vast, time is so baffling, knowledge is so constantly expanding; how can we believe in the old-fashioned God? No doubt we need a new-fashioned God, an expanding religious imagination. This task may be theological, but we deal with it whenever we pray. Who is this God who made me, who pours out love on me, who wants to offer me consolation and joy? Even in a technological age we can stretch the religious imagination. "If I take the wings of the morning, and dwell in the uttermost parts of the sea, You are there" (Psalm 139, paraphrase). The psalmist who took the wings of the morning soared far beyond the technology of his time. The God he knew about had known him in the womb, when his bones were being formed in secret.

In the wild spaces of prayer we, too, must let imagination soar, to know a God who rules the galaxies.

Metaphor

RECENTLY SOME high-technology believers were interviewed by *USA Today*.[19] Those who understood the capacity of the computer chip said it had helped them to imagine how God could stay in touch with everyone at once throughout the world and throughout the centuries. How can God suit his responses to so many? What is the technology of prayer? To understand spiritual truth we need the beauty of metaphor. Jesus taught about the reign of God with comparisons from ordinary life: yeast helping the dough to rise, seed scattered on stony ground. Twenty-first-century people can also embrace the universe and express the reality of God in contemporary terms.

Asking

....

ASKING IS BASIC TO PRAYER. Jesus taught us to pray this way. He himself used the prayer of petition. Often his requests were not small: to heal the sick, cleanse the leper, cast out devils, and raise the dead. By contrast, some teachers of prayer—Agnes Sanford is one—suggest that we ask for small things: to find lost umbrellas and misplaced tools. The simplest kind of asking requires an act of faith. Often we do not ask for things because we are afraid of a "no," a door slammed in the face. But every kind of prayer involves an "asking." When we attempt contemplation, we are asking God to be with us. Almost everything we can think of to pray about requires God's intervention, God's favor, God's concern.

Interceding

....

SEVERAL YEARS AGO I led a retreat at an ecumenical house of prayer in Richmond, Virginia. They had invited me to come and teach them about contemplative prayer, and I spent a day with them. But I think they may have taught me more about prayer than I taught them.

At given points in the day they gathered for prayer of intercession for the city of Richmond. They focused their energy on the needs of the city. There was a particular problem brewing in one part of the city, which I believe had to do with a debate over education. They prayed specifically for that, and for those who were involved in it. They prayed for the needs of the homeless, for the sick, for those who were outside of faith and who were lonely for the grace of God, for the economic needs of the city, for countless specific issues facing the residents of Richmond. I can't reconstruct it completely, since it was their city, not mine. But that's the point. They were holding up God's vision of justice and peace and love for their own city. They were praying it very intensely. Their prayer was large-minded and visionary. They reminded me not to underestimate intercessory prayer.

Praying for God's intervention on behalf of individuals and circumstances is a time-honored and deeply authentic form of prayer. Just because we learned it when we were children we should not dismiss it as "children's prayer." Our dreams for a peaceful and joyful world are pleasing to God. We should frame them by praying the prayer of intercession for all the causes we care about most. Many causes that seem limited and local are actually global. When we pray for the people of California to be spared from blackouts and brownouts, we are praying for God's hand upon the energy crisis, an issue which encircles the globe. Do we believe in a God who is powerful and loving enough to assist us in this? The prayer of intercession is an inexhaustible resource.

Repetition

THE BIBLE CAUTIONS US against empty repetition. But some repetition isn't empty. Certain prayers, like the litany, are composed in a repetitive style. Certain chants are ways of harmoniously repeating a single prayer. The Jesus prayer, "O Lord, Jesus Christ, Son of David, have mercy on me," is often a repeated prayer. Sometimes prayers of a single word, such as "Jesus" or "Lord" may lead us deeply into the presence of God. Some people find (especially in times of trouble) that repetitive prayers are comforting. If we feel moved to this kind of prayer, we should use it unselfconsciously.

Meditating

....

BOTH MEDITATION AND contemplation are forms of private prayer. Definitions for these types of prayer may vary. Sometimes it is said that meditation involves thought and reflection, while contemplation is of the heart. My experience is that whether we contemplate or meditate, we should let go of formal thought or reasoning and pray at the heart-level.

The Psalms encourage us to meditate: "I will meditate on your precepts and fix my eyes on your ways" (Ps. 119:15). Or consider the text from Philippians 2:5: "Let the same mind be in you that was in Christ Jesus." Principally this text is an encouragement to humility and love. But in another sense, to take on the mind of Jesus is to take on his practice of prayer.

As far as we know, the Hebrew style of meditation was a kind of murmuring, whispering through the words of Scripture in an attentive and prayerful way. For us today, meditation may take the form of reading a Scripture text prayerfully, then stopping to dwell on—or dwell *in*—a striking phrase or word. A refinement of this is called in Latin, *lectio divina*, which means "holy reading." You take a familiar text, read until a phrase really captures your attention, and then move "through" or beyond the text into deep or even contemplative prayer. Meditation may also take the form of reflection. I may read the story of Jesus in the Garden of Gethsemane, for example. After reading it, I may take a notebook and write down my reflections, answering the question: "How is God speaking to me through this text?" Such meditation on a text is not study, but a form of prayer. We meditate to come closer to God, to understand God's will for us, to apply the meanings of Scripture to our own lives. We meditate in order to internalize the Word and be changed by it. If meditation leads to contemplation, so much the better. All the ways of prayer are excellent ways.

Story-Meditation

....

STILL ANOTHER KIND of meditation involves
entering into a Bible story by way of the imagination. Essentially, you restage it in your mind,
becoming one or more of the characters.
Recently a young man told me how he has used
the story of Jacob wrestling with the angel in
this way. In using Gospel stories we may become
disciples of Jesus. The story of Martha and Mary
entertaining Jesus in their home at Bethany is a
very suitable story for meditation. I can become
Martha, away in the kitchen, getting everything
ready for dinner and thinking how pleased the
group will be when the meal is set before them.
Then I can hear Jesus talking in the other room,
and wish that I could sit at his feet as Mary is
doing. I can come to the door and confront
them. I can change places now and become
Mary, drinking in the words and wisdom of
Jesus in a simple way.

Works of Art

....

SOME OF US LIKE to meditate with works of art, generally with a piece of music that affects us specially, or perhaps with a painting or a photograph. Perhaps you are moved by Monet's lilies or Georgia O'Keefe's blooms. Do you have a recording that makes you prayerful? Use it. Sometimes a certain picture alerts me to an issue which lies deep. For some years now I have used a postcard reproduction of Stanley Spencer's painting, *The Resurrection, Cookham*, as part of my prayer. The painting depicts the general resurrection as it might cheerfully take place in Spencer's own home town, the English village of Cookham. The painting is profound. But more than that, praying with it gives me a chance to come to terms with my own understanding of God's love for me.

Improvising

IN FORMER TIMES many people were anxious about distractions. They blamed themselves so severely for distractions that they could hardly pray. Another way to think about prayer is as an improvisation. If we begin in a certain text, and are led to another, perhaps this is a work of grace. If a problem at the office constantly presents itself, this may need to be the subject matter of our prayer. Even a grocery list (Do I need to stop for milk on the way home?) should not annoy us, but help us to recognize the nature of our lives, built up out of a thousand small details and considerations. Bring all of yourself into prayer, and all will be well. Certain days and times will be more focused, others less. Accept this as the necessary rhythm of prayer.

Contemplating

....

CONTEMPLATION IS OFTEN thought of as an advanced form of prayer, one for which we need to qualify. Yet wanting to pray in a contemplative style may be all that is needed. In contemplation we learn to move beyond words, to gaze at God and listen. Our best model for this, apart from Jesus himself, could be Mary of Bethany, who sat at Jesus' feet and listened to his talk. In a time of silent prayer, we may focus on God. God may pour his love out on us. God may offer us compliments, he may say he is well-pleased with us. He may fill our hearts with a sense of being called. He may lift us to new levels of faith and hope. All this is contemplation.

We move into this kind of prayer by entering into the silence, going into the hush, listening for the Voice. When God speaks to us, we may respond with feelings, with affections, with answers, with delight, even with joy or bliss. In the middle of this silence, this place without words, we may enter into a conversation with God. How is this possible, if contemplation is beyond words? Thomas Merton summed it up by telling us that contemplation is all about love. He also told us that every Christian is called to contemplation and that contemplation is deeply connected to action.[20]

The prayer experience might be something like this. We come to a quiet place where prayer is possible for us. We put aside our concerns about time. We become attentive, recollected, gathered in. We enter the presence of God, we become conscious of God's presence. We allow God to speak to us, expressing love in ways that may be gentle or strong, but not a matter of polite conversation. The prayer is usually word-less. Often it is passionate.

Writers about prayer may know that such an experience is beyond description. But because they want to share the experience, they try to describe it anyway, using comparisons and metaphors, telling stories. They want to invite others to pray.

Rest

*I*S ANY NEED MORE PERVASIVE in our society than the need for rest? We hurtle from one activity to another; our work is often frenetic and rushed. Getting to and from work may be very stressful. Often, after we get home from work, we still can't rest, because we have so many personal obligations. We have to shop, prepare meals, clean up after meals, review the mail, pay the bills. Maybe we have our own schedules for exercise or obligations affecting our children: parents' meetings, civic meetings, neighborhood associations, you name it. Many of us are so wound up that when we get a chance to sleep, we can't.

Prayer restores us with a kind of rest that the business of the world takes away from us. Jesus specifically invites us to this kind of rest when he says, "Come unto me, all you that are weary and carrying heavy burdens, and I will give you rest" (Matt. 11:28). Not only do we need to come to stillness, but also we need to rest deeply in God, knowing that we can rely on God's strength and power.

Sabbath

THE GREAT WISDOM in keeping the Sabbath is more than just stopping to rest or refraining from work. It is a matter of trusting the power of God. The Creation story tells us that God worked for six days to create everything. And on the seventh day he rested. The commandment says, "Six days you shall labor and do all your work, but the seventh day is a sabbath day to the Lord Your God" (Exodus 20:8). The commandment goes on to say that you should rest, everyone in your household should rest, your animals should rest, and so forth. If you ever keep Sabbath this way, you know that it makes a demand on you. You have to let go of your computer and your cell phone and your Palm Pilot, those unpaid bills piling up on the dining room table, and the sheaf of unanswered letters collecting in the punch bowl. But why is it difficult to refrain from work? We have to let go of our sense of control. That is the underlying issue, the Sabbath-principle. God is in charge. God is running the world. The world can run

without me for at least twenty-four hours. I am
not entirely in charge to begin with, no matter
what day of the week it is. God gives me something I could never provide on my own. The
point of the Sabbath is *shalom*: the deep and
everlasting rest of God, the peace that passes all
understanding.

Sabbath-keeping is a kind of praise, not that
we voice our praise, but that we live it. We see
God's grandness and our smallness. In our little
corner of existence the beauty of God's plan
shines out. The mighty one is with us. God's
people are at peace. Each Sabbath-moment is
sacred: children chasing each other around the
sofas, babies fussing, friends arriving, the hand-
in-hand stroll through the neighborhood. In
the praying, the joking, the news-telling, in all
these concrete moments we see God. How can
we celebrate peace, when there is no peace?
The peace we honor is the peace the world
cannot give. Yet this peace that the world does
not give, this God-given peace, is for the sake
of us, for the sake of the world. Sabbath sur-
rounds us with loving boundaries. In our
celebration of the Lord's peace we know our
limits and are glad of them. "You hem me in,
behind and before," says Psalm 139. We need

this hemming-in, this sense of being surrounded by God.

The Sabbath comes to an end. Now it is no longer Saturday-Sabbath or Sunday-Lord's Day-Sabbath, but Monday. Monday is rarely anyone's favorite day. But all the days belong to God. This is the truth we celebrate when we practice the discipline of prayer. In every kind of prayer we honor the sovereignty of God. God is the foundation of our rest and the focus of our contemplation.

Difficulties

WHEN WE HIT OBSTACLES in prayer, we should look first to common sense. Is it fatigue? Stress? Lack of sleep? Lack of variety? Sometimes a change of scene may bring about a change of heart. But maybe the problem lies deeper. Way underneath, habitually, below our line of vision, we may feel neglected or unloved. Our notions of God are twisted, narrow, small. How do we swap such a tight-fisted God-idea for one that is more generous and loving? Facing our disenchantments honestly may help. In person, or in our spiritual reading, we may seek out those who have turned similar corners. Prayer often means starting over after we have been stranded or stuck. John Henry Newman in his sermon on Christian repentance says, "The most perfect Christian is ever but beginning."[21] Prayer is always a homecoming, something like that of the Prodigal Son, though the return is not always so dramatic. I like the phrase Eugene Peterson uses: "A long obedience in the same direction."[22] To shape such an obedience requires diligence, commitment, hopefulness. The gift of ourselves has to be made again. From the low-lying ocean of our discouragement, we enter a sort of passage and ascend through the locks into pacific swells of grace.

Perseverance

....

OFTEN WE START OFF bravely in prayer and are swamped at first with consolation. Later we may hit a dry period, one that seems endless, when God seems distant, indifferent, cold. To keep going in prayer at such a time takes courage. Perhaps that is why the old writers spoke of the castle of perseverance. In that noble fortress we should stop to fortify ourselves and re-learn a waiting strategy. How to hang on till help comes? It may help to take a long view. In the long run all will be well. And the waiting (though we hate to admit it) will be the making of us.

Waiting

....

IS WAITING THE worst thing about the life of prayer? Sometimes it is both the worst and the best. Say we have put in our request for something and the answer is slow. We suspect we have come up against celestial bureaucracy. Anyhow we have to wait. We hate to admit that we are deepened by this waiting. Waiting makes us strong. We thought we were frivolous, impatient people, bent on self-gratification. Slowly, we grasp what we are made of. Patience sharpens and refines us. We endure. We live at a deeper level. We serve by waiting, as Milton says of the angels. We are glad of our parts in the chorus, spear-carriers. "They also serve who only stand and wait."[23]

Depths

THOSE WHO HAVE BEEN down in diving bells report that it is terrifyingly calm. At a certain depth in our own lives the spiritual pressure becomes severe. We may feel we are prisoners of the psyche, lost in some hellish region where no light shines. Out of this unspeakable depth I cry to you, Lord. Hear my prayer. Increase my fidelity. Maintain my air supply. Let me know this darkness is not dark to you, to you it is the light of day.

Heights

SOMETIMES WE ARE GRACED with euphoria in prayer. We feel like spiritual giants wearing seven-league boots. In our prayer we have crossed a continent and look out on the western sea. It is grand, it is mystical, it is ineffable, it is beyond space and time, it is not guaranteed. Even to speak of it may be to land with a thud. Did we dream it all? Yet we know such things are possible. In Genesis 15:12, ". . . a deep sleep fell on Abram, and a deep and terrifying darkness descended upon him," when the Lord showed him the oppression that would come to his people at a future time. As Moses came down from the mountain after his direct encounter with God, he did not know how intensely his face was shining. But in Exodus 34:30 we read, "When Aaron and all the Israelites saw Moses . . . they were afraid to come near him." The face of Moses had to be veiled for a time. Jesus also was transfigured in prayer. Paul was caught up into the third heaven.

Almost always, to be at the heights is to return with a bigger vision of what God wants for his people and from us. No wonder we are sometimes afraid of heights.

Transformation

CONTEMPLATIVE EXPERIENCE may change us. The Christian psychiatrist Gerald May has identified a number of ways it may do so. He says we may gain clarity and breadth of awareness. Instead of shifting our attention back and forth among different tasks as we used to do, now we have a larger attention span. Contemplatives develop more panoramic, all-inclusive awareness. We are less bothered by distractions.

Second, we are more responsive to situations. We become more centered in the present and more capable of taking decisive action here and now. We can respond to the unexpected.

Third, we know ourselves better. As we gain in self knowledge, we are less subject to many existential anxieties. In short, the habit of deep prayer brings us into a kind of freedom. It strengthens us.[24] I believe that a further effect of this kind of prayer is that we become more compassionate.

Spiritual Direction

....

THE ANCIENT DISCIPLINE of spiritual direction, once confined to religious communities, is now used broadly by lay people as well. Meetings with a trained director, weekly, monthly, or at longer intervals, may help us to sustain a regular commitment to prayer. In the meetings we describe our prayer experiences, our joys and difficulties, and gain perspective on how prayer may be shaping us. The spiritual director helps us to develop confidence in God, to relax in prayer, to deal with trouble spots of any kind. Spiritual direction is not entirely professionalized, but there are now many trained directors. The director should be a person experienced in prayer and able to listen.

Spiritual direction can become a deeply valued aspect of our prayer lives. Sometimes these relationships take on the character of friendships. However, as long as the direction is in progress, maintaining a certain holy distance is good. Keep confidentiality, both for your sake and the director's. As with retreats, spiritual direction is a work of the Holy Spirit. Honor and treasure it as such.

Unceasing Prayer

PAUL TOLD THE THESSALONIAN Christians to pray without ceasing. Sometimes we interpret this counsel, in 1 Thessalonians 5:17, as an impossible task. We imagine prayer as hard work, and say to ourselves, "I can't be always praying." That's what's so good about the life of contemplation. It isn't really about hard work. It's about resting in God. And floating free.

When I was a child I always wanted an English bike like the one my friend Sidney had. His was light as a feather—Raleigh was the brand as I recall—while I was stuck with a ponderous, heavyweight Schwinn. The advantage of his bike was that if you pedaled part of the time, you didn't have to pedal all of the time. At a certain moment when you had built up some power, you could let go and the bike would carry you along. The prayer-filled life is like that.

Is loving God hard or easy? It is easy to those who do it. When we become contemplatives, we are in the process of being changed, but we ourselves don't notice the transformation. We can see it in others, and others can see it in us.

Of course there are pitfalls in describing the attractions of prayer. Others object that it can't be that easy! People of prayer and those who write about it know that the life of prayer is unique to each person and will probably be both hard and easy.

"Unceasing prayer" is prayer that becomes part and parcel of us and changes us in noticeable ways.

Paul, in his Letters, has much to say about the changes that God will work in us. He speaks passionately of the way we will come to love each other. He waxes eloquent about spiritual friendship. He challenges us to give way to the love of God that we experience when we pray.

So in prayer we begin to develop a different world vision. Fueled by grace, we refuse to stay on the sidelines. Prayer helps us to believe things can be different. Through a mystery, prayer is linked to action, not simply by our own intentions, but by the grace and the will of God.

Blessedness

....

A QUICK LOOK at the sayings of Jesus should give us a hint of what prayer will accomplish in our lives. Blessedness, or union with God, will alter the way we perceive things. We will become people who are willing to be persecuted, to take chances, to trust that our mourning will be turned into dancing. Still, this blessedness comes while we are still engaged in the struggle. Prayer strengthens us, but doesn't exempt us from life's pressures. A certain wrestling with God, a reaching to find God's will, is part of what we may expect in prayer. The honeymoon moments will come and go. Sometimes there will be only waiting, and watching. At the same time we can count on the grace of it, even a certain sweetness. Secretly, we are in touch with a God who knows our hearts. God will go with us on the journey. All will be well.

So we may come to accept a life lived in another dimension, a love that warms us, a power that befriends us in trouble. What the old spiritual writers call "union" possesses us completely. Although sometimes we may be caught up in passionate love-chat, more often we move through our nights and days surrounded by God's care. It is a secret that can hardly be told, though we try to tell it. The old stories of Moses on the mountain and Elijah's chariot make sense in ways we can hardly convey. It is a closeness, it is a passion, it is a refining fire. Words fail us, and we live out the joy of prayer life mostly not trying to explain. Others may wonder what moves us so, and why we think this way. Loud evangelizing is hardly our style, but we try to bear witness, by what we say or do, to a grace that passes understanding.

Exercises

Exercises
for Prayer

I BELIEVE THAT PRAYER can be creative, a collage of the readings and types of prayer that please and sustain us. In that spirit I offer some suggestions here, brief maps of ways that prayer time might be well used. I hope you will find them useful starting points, even "frames" for your own ways of praying.

Please note that each suggested exercise calls for a certain time period of prayer. Also, each exercise calls for a somewhat different prayer method. No doubt you will create variations by using different Scriptures, or by designing exercises of your own.

Build variety into the prayer time. Move your location. Take a walk or sit outside if the weather permits. You might pause from time to time. Move beyond thought and reflection toward simply being in the presence of God.

Psalm 139 *(Twenty Minutes)*

The intent here is to appreciate the mightiness of God, and God's care and concern for us. To do this, we'll use a large part of Psalm 139, which describes not only the power of God, but also God's intimate friendship and closeness to us at every minute of day and night, from the beginning of our lives in the womb, wherever we live, whether we travel in far-distant places or close to home.

Yahweh, you examine me and know me,
you know if I am standing or sitting,
you read my thoughts from far away,
whether I walk or lie down, you are watching,
you know every detail of my conduct.

The word is not even on my tongue,
Yahweh, before you know all about it;
close behind and close in front you fence me round,
shielding me with your hand.
Such knowledge is beyond my understanding,
a height to which my mind cannot attain.

Where could I go to escape your spirit?
Where could I flee from your presence?
If I climb the heavens, you are there,
there, too, if I lie in Sheol.

If I flew to the point of sunrise,
or westward across the sea,
your right hand would still be guiding me,
your right hand holding me.

If I asked darkness to cover me,
and light to become night around me,
that darkness would not be dark to you,
night would be as light as day.

It was you who created my inmost self,
and put me together in my mother's womb;
for all these mysteries I thank you:
for the wonder of myself, for the wonder of your
works.

You know me through and through,
from having watched my bones take shape
when I was being formed in secret,
knitted together in the limbo of the womb.

You had scrutinised my every action,
all were recorded in your book,
my days listed and determined,
even before the first of them occurred.

God, how hard it is to grasp your thoughts!
How impossible to count them!
I could no more count them than I could the sand,
and suppose I could, you would still be with me.

God, examine me and know my heart,
probe me and know my thoughts;
make sure I do not follow pernicious ways,
and guide me in the way that is everlasting.

(Psalm 139:1–18, 23–24 JB)

If you prefer to use your own Bible, please do so.

One way to pray this psalm is by the method called lectio divina, sacred reading. You read through the whole psalm quietly and prayerfully, letting God become very present to you as you read. As you read the psalm over several times, one phrase will become very important to you. Put another way, you will choose a phrase that strikes you prayerfully.

Move into the presence of the Lord through this phrase, whispering the phrase to yourself, repeating the phrase mentally, or holding the phrase in your mind. "You know me through and through." "Guide me in the way that is everlasting."

Or you may paraphrase the thoughts of the psalm, using your own words: "With all my ways you are familiar." "You know me, Lord." "You hold me."

Rest in the presence of God in this simple phrase. Then, when you feel called to do this, move into the presence of God beyond the text. Rest in the presence of God. Feel God's love and tenderness to you. Be conscious of God's power and protection.

This is no time to question anything. Instead, let worry and anxiety slide away. Be at peace.

Song of Moses and Miriam *(Twenty–Thirty Minutes)*

This exercise combines scriptural meditation with contemplative prayer, using the song of Moses and his sister Miriam in Exodus 15:1–21. This is one of the many formal songs in Scripture, also known as canticles, in which God's power is being praised because of a particular event or deliverance. Moses, Miriam, and the Israelites, after long years of enslavement in Egypt, have been delivered from the oppression of Pharaoh and are on their way back to their home country. They have passed safely through the Red Sea, looking at a high wall of water on either side of them, but walking on solid ground. After their passage, Pharaoh's pursuing chariots are swamped and destroyed as the waters close in again. Moses and Miriam—both referred to as prophets—are rejoicing in the deliverance of their people.

During your prayer time, place yourself with Moses, Miriam, and the people of God, on the seashore. They have come through a monstrous challenge unscathed; they want to praise God and make a new start. Miriam, the prophet, takes a tambourine in her hand and leads the people in a joyful dance (Exodus 15:20). Spiritually, this is a time for dancing and rejoicing. Identify with this spirit of thanksgiving as you read.

I will sing to the LORD, for he
has triumphed gloriously;
horse and rider he has thrown
into the sea.
The LORD is my strength and my might,
and he has become my salvation;
this is my God, and I will praise him,
my father's God, and I will exalt him.
The LORD is a warrior;
the LORD is his name.

(Exodus 15:1–3)

Pause here, and recall the ways that God has delivered you in the past. Treasure your own reasons for rejoicing. Unite yourself with Moses and Miriam in their celebration.

Who is like you, O LORD, among the gods?
Who is like you, majestic in holiness,
awesome in splendor, doing wonders?

(Exodus 15:11)

In your steadfast love you led the people
whom you redeemed;
you guided them by your strength to
your holy abode.

(Exodus 15: 13)

You brought them in and planted them
on the mountain of your own possession,
the place, O Lord, that you made your abode;
the sanctuary, O Lord, that
your hands have established.
The Lord will reign forever and ever.

(Exodus 15: 17–18)

Pray this canticle as your personal prayer. You may do this silently or by whispering the words to yourself under your breath. At the end of the canticle, or at any point during the canticle, enter "through the text" into the divine presence.

Find a short phrase that touches you: "This is my God," or "I will praise him," or "Who is like you, O Lord?" Pray the phrase until it leads you beyond words. At the end of the prayer period, close with these words: "The Lord will reign forever and ever."

THIRD EXERCISE:

A Gospel Encounter

(One Hour or More)

You will need a Bible for this exercise, because you'll be reading parts of the Gospel of Matthew: Chapters 5, 6, and 7. This section of the Gospel is often referred to as the Sermon on the Mount. In reading it, you may wish to imagine yourself as one of the disciples who followed Jesus from town to town, or who gathered in a particular locality to hear him during his preaching ministry. You can see yourself—dusty, hot, tired from the journey—sitting down on the ground as one of those who came to hear an exciting and spirit-filled Teacher and Healer from Galilee, whose fame was growing far and wide. Receive into your heart the distilled wisdom of the things that Jesus has to say.

Instead of being just one of the crowd, choose to identify with one of the well-known disciples who followed Jesus, who are mentioned in the Gospel by name. Consider whether you want to place yourself in the scene as Peter or James or John, as Mary of Bethany, or Mary the Mother of Jesus. "Becoming" one of these disciples may help you to see your vocation in

terms of the human frailties of these remarkable people, or to appropriate some of their
courage and strength.

As you read, also keep the question of contemporary discipleship in mind. What does it
mean to follow Jesus today? What is Jesus asking
or expecting of twenty-first-century disciples?

The method I would suggest is as follows:
Read through the three chapters in a leisurely
manner. Your task here is not to study the text,
but to allow Jesus to become present to you. If
anything strikes you, stop for prayer or a time of
reflection. You may write about your prayer
experience during this time, but be sure to give
the experience its full weight before stopping to
capture it in your journal. But do what works for
you! This should be a creative and blessed time.

For prayer, concentrate on Matthew 6:1–13,
in which Jesus teaches his disciples how to pray.
Use the text of the prayer as it is given in the
Gospel for your prayer. This may differ slightly
from the Lord's Prayer as we generally say it. In
the New Revised Standard Version the text of
the prayer reads:

Our Father in heaven,
hallowed be your name.
Your kingdom come.
Your will be done,
on earth as it is in heaven.
Give us this day our daily bread.
And forgive us our debts,
as we also have forgiven our debtors.
And do not bring us to the time of trial,
But rescue us from the evil one.

Pray through this prayer line by line, taking time after each intention to experience the full meaning of the prayer.

Possibly, in reading the Gospel chapters and doing the exercise just ended, you will have completed your hour. But if time remains, try a second text for prayer: Matthew 7:7–11 and Matthew 7:13–14. Jesus says: "Ask, and it will be given you; search, and you will find; knock, and the door will be opened for you. For everyone who asks receives, and everyone who searches finds, and for everyone who knocks, the door will be opened. Is there anyone among you who, if your child asks for bread, will give a stone? Or if the child asks for a fish, will give a snake? If you then, who are evil, know how to give good gifts to your children, how much more will your Father in heaven give good things to those who ask him!" A moment later Jesus adds, "Enter through the narrow gate; for the gate is wide and the road is easy that leads to destruction, and there are many who take it. For the gate is narrow and the road is hard that leads to life, and there are few who find it."

Perhaps you have studied these teachings before. In this exercise, instead of studying them, we are praying them. When Jesus says "enter through the narrow gate," he is speaking, not only about righteousness, but also about prayer, and prayer is sometimes referred to as "the narrow way." Pray yourself through the narrow gate, into the blessed presence of God.

At the end of the prayer time, reflect on your relationship with Jesus. What is Jesus saying to you in the prayer time? What sense of his presence can you take along with you as the prayer time ends?

The Warehouse
of My Soul *(Twenty Minutes)*

Read the following selection from Karl Rahner's prayer, "God of My Daily Routine."

(Dear God) My soul has become a huge warehouse where day after day the trucks unload their crates without any plan or discrimination, to be piled helter-skelter in every available corner and cranny, until it is crammed full from top to bottom with the trite, the commonplace, the insignificant, the routine. . . .

Empty talk and pointless activity, idle curiosity and pretensions of importance that . . . roll forward in a never-ending stream.

I now see clearly that, if there is any path at all on which I can approach You, it must lead through the middle of my ordinary daily life. . . .

I must learn to have both "everyday" and Your Day in the same exercise. In devoting myself to the works of this world, I must learn to give myself to You, to possess You, the one and only thing, in everything. . . .

Before You, all multiplicity becomes one; in You,
all that has been scattered is reunited; in Your Love
all the diffusion of the day's chores comes home
again to the evening of Your unity. . . .

After reading the prayer, close your eyes and
spend a brief time in silent prayer, no more than
five minutes. During your prayer, place yourself
in the presence of God. Be conscious of God's
love for you and his appreciation of all the kinds
of work you do.

When you open your eyes, write a brief list of
all the sources of tension in your work life. For
example, you might write: "Too many phone
calls," "Having to work overtime, or working
too long hours," or "Not enough time for my
family." When you have listed several of these,
stop.

Now pray again, seeing God (Father, Son,
Holy Spirit) present to you in each of these trying situations. Be open to God's love for you in
your work. Imagine God blessing you in your
work, blessing your hands on the computer
keys, or accompanying you during a stressful
rush hour when traffic may be backed up on the
freeway. Experience the power of God sustain-
ing you in your daily struggles. Conclude by

praying (out loud, or silently) the words of Philippians 4:13, "I can do all things through him who strengthens me."

For a Change of Heart *(Twenty Minutes)*

These reflection questions are meant to call you more deeply to conversion. The method is to read each question, pray briefly about it, then answer that question briefly before moving to the next. Take as much time as you need with each question. If you find that, after the prayer period, you have dealt with only one or two of the questions, well and good. Come back to the questions again another time.

- What am I passionate for?
- What kind of leverage do I have in my community or profession?
- Does my work express what I genuinely believe and value?
- Am I using my real gifts and talents to benefit myself and others?
- Am I in the middle of a shift of consciousness, being called beyond my present work to something that will more perfectly express my sense of calling?
- What are my first principles, the things from which I won't depart?
- Am I living according to these principles?

- How do I deal with darkness and discouragement?
- Have I considered the possibility that God has a serious large-scale task in mind for me, something for which I am well qualified?
- What about the power of persuasion in my life: Have I set out to persuade anyone of the merits of a good cause? Am I open to using my personal persuasive gifts? Am I open to persuasion from others for the sake of God's kingdom?
- Have I personally set an initiative in motion that will change the status quo? Is there an initiative I should start, or join, that takes on large-scale issues with a view to courageous change?
- Is it time for a change of heart? In what way?

At the end of your prayer period, close with these words from Luke 1:37:

For nothing will be impossible with God.

This short declaration is what the angel said to Mary when he told her about the wonderful child she would bring into the world. We, too, can use it to express our trust that God will do great things through us.

Please feel free to use these brief exercises as a creative stimulus. Use them, or invent others that work well for you. While prayer should have definite shape and structure, it also needs to be spontaneous and from the heart. Adapting these exercises, making them your own, will soon have you turning cartwheels before God.

Blessings on your prayer!

Afterword

....

Read and Be Glad: Suggested Reading

BOOKS MAY LEAD US into prayer, strengthen our resolve, answer our questions, give us hope in times of doubt.

Here are a few of my own favorites. William Barry, a well-known spiritual director, has written many good books. Among these I especially like *What Do I Want in Prayer?* (New York: Paulist Press, 1994). This book helps in focusing our prayer intentions. A rich exploration of many types of prayer is found in Richard Foster's *Prayer: Finding the Heart's True Home* (San Francisco, Harper San Francisco, 1992). Timothy Jones introduces us to prayer in a fresh, personal way in *The Art of Prayer: A Simple Guide* (New York: Ballantine, 1997). James Bryan Smith has written a moving book on how we can more deeply accept God's love in prayer, called *Embracing the Love of God* (San Francisco, Harper San Francisco, 1995). I like Mark Thibodeaux's book, *Armchair Mystic: Easing into Contemplative Prayer* (Cincinnati, OH: St. Anthony Messenger

Press, 2001). Gregory and Suzanne Wolfe have written a book about family prayer. Focused on ways to teach children to pray, their book is a fine commentary on prayer for everyone: *Circle of Grace* (New York: Ballantine, 2001).

A useful guide for lectio divina is Thelma Hall's, *Too Deep for Words: Rediscovering Lectio Divina* (New York: Paulist Press, 1988). This instructive book includes 500 Scripture texts for prayer. Basil Pennington's book *Centering Prayer: Renewing an Ancient Christian Prayer Form* (New York: Doubleday Image, 1982) also teaches lectio divina together with great wisdom about contemplation. Pennington is a Cistercian monk, and Cistercian writers, whose prayer is shaped by vows of silence, are excellent prayer guides. Consider Andre Louf, who has two brief popular works, *Teach Us to Pray: Learning a Little About God* (New York: Paulist Press, 1975) and *The Cistercian Way* (Kalamazoo, MI: Cistercian Publications, 1983). Louf, who lives at the Katzberg monastery in Belgium, is principally writing for monks. But the lightness and beauty of his teaching can easily be applied outside of cloister walls.

Thomas Merton is a major Cistercian writer who has made prayer accessible to many. I especially like *Contemplative Prayer* (New York: Doubleday, 1971) and *New Seeds of Contemplation* (New York: Doubleday, 1974).

Evelyn Underhill is considered an important writer on the mystical life. Two short, but pithy, works of hers are: *Practical Mysticism* (New York: E.P. Dutton, first published 1915) and *The Spiritual Life* (New York, Harper & Row, no date). I recommend anything by Henri Nouwen, but one treasure of a book is his *The Way of the Heart: Desert Spirituality and Contemporary Ministry* (New York: HarperCollins, 1981).

Don't overlook C.S. Lewis, *Letters to Malcolm: Chiefly on Prayer* (New York: Harcourt Brace Jovanovich, 1964). This brief work focuses mostly on petition and intercession. But it also offers sound insights on the whole practice of prayer.

Luci Shaw has written movingly in poetry and prose. I like her book about journaling, *Life Path* (Portland, Oregon: Multnomah, 1991) and *Water My Soul* (Grand Rapids, MI: Zondervan, 1999). Jeanie Miley also writes beautifully about prayer, including such useful books as *The Spiritual Art of Creative Silence: Lessons in Christian Meditation* (Wheaton, IL: Harold Shaw, 1996).

How could I fail to mention Annie Dillard? She does not instruct about prayer, but her transparent writing shows the deep insight gained from meditative living. I am thinking especially of such works as *The Writing Life* (New York: HarperCollins, 1998), and *Teaching A Stone to Talk* (New York: Harper & Row, 1982).

I would also like to commend to the reader my own book on prayer, *Clinging: The Experience of Prayer* (New York: McCracken Press, 1994). This brief work explores seven aspects of prayer

I remember a children's verse that says, "Books are paths that upward lead." I hope so! May this little book of mine and many others become doors of invitation for you. Keep the Bible close by and explore it as your first source-book on prayer. Pray often, in the way that comes easiest. Enjoy the presence of God. Be glad of God's love and power. Lift up your heart and be drenched by cloudbursts of grace.

Endnotes

1. A. A. Milne, *When We Were Very Young* (New York: E. P. Dutton & Co., Inc., 1924), 101–102.

2. Thomas Merton, *The Seven Storey Mountain* (Garden City, New York: Doubleday Image Books, 1970), 19.

3. C.S. Lewis, *Surprised by Joy: the Shape of My Early Life* (New York: Harcourt Brace Jovanovich, 1955), 7.

4. Blaise Pascal, "Thoughts," given in *The Oxford Dictionary of Quotations*, Second Edition (London: Oxford University Press, 1955), 374.

5. Evelyn Underhill, *The Spiritual Life* (New York: Harper & Row, no date), 61. Underhill uses the phrase "incurable God-sickness," which she attributes to Karl Barth.

6. Augustine, *Confessions*, John K. Ryan, trans. (Garden City, New York: Doubleday Image Books, 1960), 43.

7. Dorothy Day, *The Long Loneliness* (Chicago: Thomas More Press, 1981).

8. William Shakespeare, *As You Like It*, Act II, Scene 1, line 15.

9. See Richard Foster, *Prayer: Finding the Heart's True Home* (San Francisco: Harper San Francisco, 1992), 161.

10. Ibid., 172.

11. Pierre Teilhard de Chardin, *The Divine Milieu* (New York: Harper & Row, 1960), 33.

12. The account of Simone Weil's experience on the Thibon farm is given in George A. Panichas, *The Simone Weil Reader* (New York: David McKay, 1977), Essay, "Concerning the Our Father," 492.

13. Janice Brewi and Anne Brennan, *Celebrate Mid-Life: Jungian Archetypes and Mid-Life Spirituality*, (New York: Crossroad, 1988), 249.

14. David Lonsdale, "The Contemplative in Everyday Life," *The Way Supplement*, No. 59, "Contemplation and the Contemplative Life" (London: The Way, 1987), 84.

15. Karl Rahner, *Encounters with Silence* (London: Sands and Co., 1960), 45–52.

16. Brother Lawrence of the Resurrection, cited in Richard Foster, *Prayer: Finding the Heart's True Home*, 124.

17. Gerard Manley Hopkins, quoted by Kathleen Norris in *The Quotidian Mysteries: Laundry, Liturgy and Women's Work* (New York: Paulist, 1998), 70–71.

18. Evelyn Underhill, *The Spiritual Life*, (New York: Harper & Row, no date), 84.

19. "Great Minds Reflect on How God Fits Into the Equation," *USA Today*, Tuesday, March 27, 2001, 1B–2B.

20. See Thomas Merton's *New Seeds of Contemplation*, (New York: New Directions, 1961), chapter one, "What is Contemplation?" 1–5.

21. John Henry Newman, *Parochial and Plain Sermons*, Vol. III (London: Longmans, Green & Co., 1899), 90.

22. Eugene Peterson, *A Long Obedience in the Same Direction* (Downers Grove, IL: Intervarsity, 1980).

23. John Milton, Sonnet "On His Blindness" is given as Sonnet XIX in Harry Francis Fletcher, ed., *The Complete Poetical Works of John Milton* (Boston: Houghton Mifflin, 1941), 134.

24. See Gerald G. May, "To Bear the Beams of Love: Contemplation and Personal Growth," in *The Way Supplement: Contemplation and the Contemplative Life*, No. 59, 24–34.

About Paraclete Press

Who We Are

Paraclete Press is an ecumenical publisher of books on Christian spirituality for people of all denominations and backgrounds.

We publish books that represent the wide spectrum of Christian belief and practice—Catholic, Orthodox, and Protestant.

We market our books primarily through booksellers; we are what is called a "trade" publisher, which means that we like it best when readers buy our books from booksellers, our partners in successfully reaching as wide an audience as possible.

We are uniquely positioned in the marketplace without connection to a large corporation or conglomerate and with informal relationships to many branches and denominations of faith, rather than a formal relationship to any single one. We focus on publishing a diversity of thoughts and perspectives—the fruit of our diversity as a company.

What We Are Doing

Paraclete Press is publishing books that show the diversity and depth of what it means to be Christian. We publish books that reflect the Christian experience across many cultures, time periods, and houses of worship.

We publish books about spiritual practice, history, ideas, customs, and rituals, and books that nourish the vibrant life of the church.

We have several different series of books within Paraclete Press, including the bestselling Living Library series of modernized classic texts, A Voice from the Monastery—giving voice to men and women monastics on what it means to live a spiritual life today, and Many Mansions—for exploring the riches of the world's religious traditions and discovering how other faiths inform Christian thought and practice.

Learn more about us at our Web site:
www.paracletepress.com, or call us toll-free at
1-800-451-5006.

The Illumined Heart:
The Ancient Christian Path of
Transformation
Frederica Mathewes-Green

112 pages
ISBN: 1-55725-286-6
$13.95 Hardcover

Why are modern Christians so indistinguishable from everyone else? Why don't they stand out in virtue and joy? How could the early saints pray constantly, fast valiantly, and love their enemies?

Today's Christianity has come untethered from its historic roots, says Frederica Mathewes-Green, yet we can recover its power by reviving this ancient, transcultural faith. Drawing on Christian writings throughout the early centuries, Mathewes-Green explores prayer, fasting, and alms-giving as aids to "theosis"—total transformation in Christ.

"As always, Frederica Mathewes-Green cuts through the niceties, the comfortable feel-good pap, the tempting cliches, to offer a hard, bold challenge: to live the Christian life as Christ meant it to be lived."
Lauren Winner, author of *Girl Meets God* and *Mudhouse Sabbath*

"Frederica Mathewes-Green is a marvelous story teller and every searcher's best friend."
Amy Dickinson, *Time* magazine

"I believe the *The Illumined Heart* will be of great help to anyone striving to walk the timeless path of Christ in our time."
Dallas Willard, author of *The Divine Conspiracy*